LEARN FRENCH
WITH THE PUMBLECHUMS

DAY TWO

BY KIERAN BALL

ISBN: 978 1 5201 5151 9

 Bonjour and welcome to another beautiful day. Blue has got up bright and early and eager to start his next French lesson with Victoria.

Here comes Victoria now. She wonders if Blue might like to do a lesson at the park today. The sun is shining and it's so warm outside. Blue says "oui", which means "yes" in French.

Blue and Victoria are heading to the park. On their way, Victoria teaches Blue a very long word in French. "Absolument". Can you guess what it means?

"How do you say it?"

Here's how you say the word "absolument" in French

absolument = "ab-soloo-mon"

You don't say the letter T on the end

 Did you guess that it means "absolutely"? Well done!

absolutely

 Victoria has stopped to ask Blue how he would say "it is absolutely fantastic" in French. Can you help him?

Did you get it right? Well done! Victoria said Blue should try saying the sentence out loud three times in French. This will help him to get better at speaking.

c'est absolument fantastique

 Victoria wonders if Blue could make the sentence a little longer. She's asked him to say in French "it is absolutely fantastic here". Can you help him again?

 Did you get that one right? Well done if you did, it was a very long one!

c'est absolument fantastique ici

 Blue and Victoria are carrying on to the park now and Blue has asked Victoria a question. He asked, "If c'est means 'it is', how do you say 'it is not'?"

Victoria says you say "ce n'est pas" and it can mean any of these three phrases:

it is not

it isn't

it's not

Blue is saying "ce n'est pas" out loud.

ce n'est pas

"How do you say it?"

Here's how you say the phrase "ce n'est pas" in French

ce n'est pas = "snay pa"

Victoria has given Blue three sentences to say in French on their way to the park using the phrase "ce n'est pas". See if you can help him...

"it isn't good"

_____

"it isn't here"

_____

"it isn't good here"

_____

 Did you get them all right?
Well done!

"it isn't good"

ce n'est pas bon

"it isn't here"

ce n'est pas ici

"it isn't good here"

ce n'est pas bon ici

 Blue and Victoria have finally got to the park and Victoria has a surprise picnic for Blue.

 Blue wants to say "thank you" to Victoria. Can you remember how to say "thank you" in French?

If you can't quite remember a word in French, never worry! It's normal to forget things when we're learning. Just go back to the last book and check.

 Well remembered!

merci

Victoria has given Blue a new word and she wants him to guess what it means. The new word is "délicieux". What do you think it means?

"How do you say it?"

Here's how you say the word "délicieux" in French

délicieux = "day-liss-yer"

You can't hear the letter X on the end.

 It means "delicious". Did you guess it right? Well done if you did.

delicious

 Victoria is asking Blue how he would say in French, "it is delicious". Can you help him by writing it on the line below?

_____

 Did you get it right?
Victoria said Blue should say it out loud
a few times.

c'est délicieux

 Victoria has asked Blue to say "it is absolutely delicious" in French as he eats his cake. Can you help him?

 That cake must have been absolument délicieux because it's all gone!

c'est absolument délicieux

Blue is full and tired. He wants to take a nap. However, Victoria has another word she wants to teach him. This word is a very small word, "ça" and it means "that"

"How do you say it?"

Here's how you say the word "ça" in French

ça = "ssa"

The letter ç is pronounced like an s

She said if you put "ça" with "c'est", you get "ça c'est". It means "that is".

ça c'est...

"How do you say it?"

Here's how you say the phrase "ça c'est" in French

ça c'est = "ssa say"

The letter ç is pronounced like an s

Victoria has asked Blue to say "that is good" in French. Can you help him out?

 Did you get it right? Well done if you did.

ça c'est bon

Now Victoria has asked Blue if he can say "that is fantastic". Can you write it on the line below?

———————————————————————

 Well done if you managed to get that one right!

ça c'est fantastique

 It's time for Blue to go home now. He's saying "thank you" to Victoria again for the picnic. It was "délicieux". Victoria said "you're welcome".

Blue helped Victoria to pack away the picnic and now he is saying goodbye. In French, "au revoir" means "goodbye".

au revoir

"How do you say it?"

Here's how you say the phrase "au revoir" in French

au revoir = "oh-re-vwar"

Victoria has just told Blue to wait a second because she has forgotten to give him a card for today's new words.

 On one side of his card, Blue has written all the English words from today's lesson with Victoria...

absolutely
it isn't
delicious
that
that is
goodbye

Then, on the other side of the card, he has written all the same words in French.

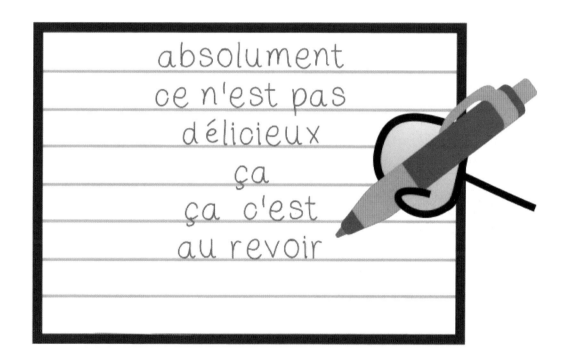

absolument
ce n'est pas
délicieux
ça
ça c'est
au revoir

Victoria has left some homework for Blue to do. Can you help him write all these sentences in French? You can turn back and use the card to help.

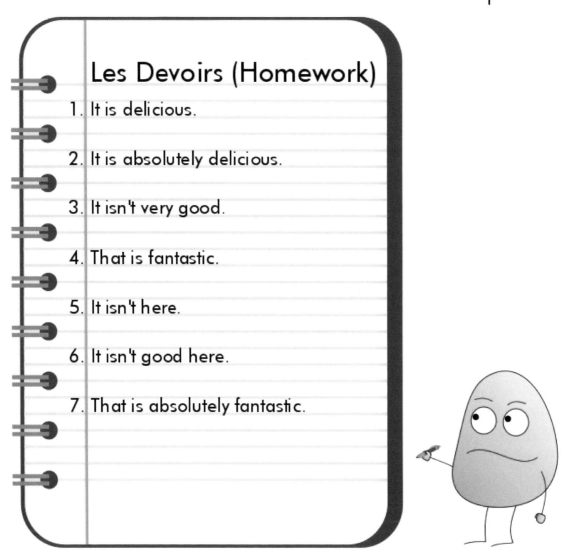

Les Devoirs (Homework)

1. It is delicious.

2. It is absolutely delicious.

3. It isn't very good.

4. That is fantastic.

5. It isn't here.

6. It isn't good here.

7. That is absolutely fantastic.

Here are all the words you will need from today's lesson.

délicieux
delicious

absolument
absolutely

ce n'est pas
it isn't

ça c'est
that is

Did you get them all right? If you did, you can go back and tick all your answers. Well done!

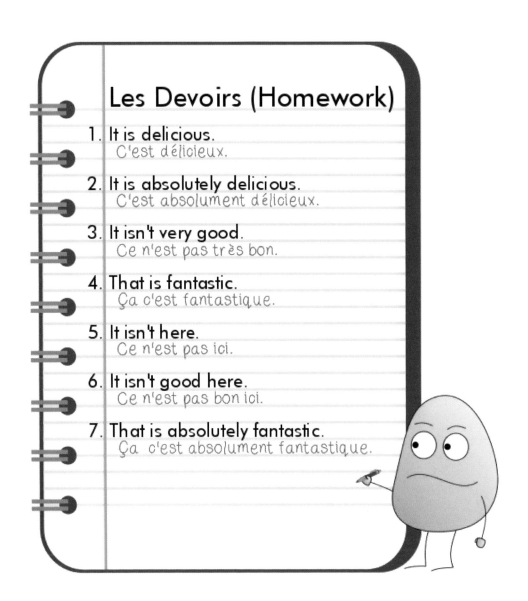

Les Devoirs (Homework)

1. It is delicious.
   C'est délicieux.

2. It is absolutely delicious.
   C'est absolument délicieux.

3. It isn't very good.
   Ce n'est pas très bon.

4. That is fantastic.
   Ça c'est fantastique.

5. It isn't here.
   Ce n'est pas ici.

6. It isn't good here.
   Ce n'est pas bon ici.

7. That is absolutely fantastic.
   Ça c'est absolument fantastique.

 Blue is now ready to go home after another long day of learning. He's saying goodbye to you...

Printed in Great Britain
by Amazon